Sulla

The Good Man Who Doomed Rome

In60Learning

Copyright © 2019 In60Learning

All rights reserved.

Sign up for the LearningList to receive

eBooks and Audiobooks

at
www.in60Learning.com
Smarter in 60 minutes.

in60Learning.com

CONTENTS

	Acknowledgments	i
1	Early Years	1
2	The Roman Republic	4
3	Early Political Career	8
4	Fighting for Power	12
5	Road to Rome	18
6	Dictator of Rome	23
7	Later Years & Legacy	28

1 EARLY YEARS

"When he was a youth, he lived in lodgings, at a low price, and this was afterwards thrust in his teeth when men thought him unduly prosperous. For instance, we are told that when he was putting on boastful airs after his campaign in Libya, a certain nobleman said to him: "How canst thou be an honest man, when thy father left thee nothing, and yet thou art so rich?"' -Plutarch, *Life of Sylla*

Lucius Cornelius Sulla Felix, known today and commonly throughout history as Sulla, was one of the greatest Roman generals and statesman who lived. He was both a consul twice and a dictator — a position in Ancient Rome which carried much different connotations than it does today. He was an accomplished general and received the highest of military honors for his service. He was involved with a series of defining political struggles within Rome and oversaw reforms to the Roman Constitution. In many ways, he set some precedents that leaders like Julius Caesar would follow when they sought to solidify more power and control over the Republic.

Sulla was born to Lucius Cornelius Sulla and an unknown mother. His grandfather was Publius Cornelius Sulla, and had been born into the patrician class but by the time Sulla was born his family was almost entirely impoverished. Not having money, Sulla cavorted with Rome's actors, lutenists, dancers, and other comedians, a habit that would stay with him for the rest of his life. He liked to be among the artists, even if they were considered of a lower class and moral standing than the rest of Roman society Through some means or another, Sulla acquired a good education, as he was said to be both well-read and fluent in Greek which only those who had been tutored well were able to do. This education may have come from open-form learning or from familial tutoring, as even though his family was poor they had a history of being well-taught and could have passed this information on. Sulla would later in life, through again unclear means, inherit a fortune that would help him climb the ladder of Roman society. According to Plutarch, this included an inheritance from his father's second wife, and a "low-born but rich unmarried lady." who may have been his mother (though in this case he would have been born extramaritally).

In 112 B.C.E. the Jugurthine War began when the grandson of Massinissa of Numidia, Jugurtha, claimed Numidia in defiance of Rome's decrees which had divided it between several members of the Numidian royal family. Rome then declared war on Jugurtha in 111 B.C.E., but was meeting with no success in the battles. Quintus Caecilius Metellus, the general in charge of the Roman legions, was wildly successful. Gaius Marius was one of his many lieutenants and saw this as an opportunity to seize power for himself. He spread rumors of defeat and incompetence to the tax collectors, or *publicani*, knowing that tax collectors were one of the best ways to spread rumors throughout the Republic as they traveled to all of its edges. The people began to call for Metellus to be removed and in 107 B.C.E. Gaius Marius replaced him as consul. Sulla was nominated as one of his officials, serving directly under him.

Gaius Marius himself did not change much of the attack plan from Metellius'. The Numidians were eventually defeated in 106 B.C.E., but this was largely due to Sulla. Sulla persuaded Jugurtha's father-in-law King Bocchus I to betray Jugurtha when he fled to the Boccus' nearby kingdom of Mauretania for refuge. It was an incredibly dangerous mission, as Sulla had to meet with the king in person to negotiate the betrayal, and throughout the event Bocchus seriously considered handing Sulla over to Jugurtha. However, in the end, he managed to sway the King to his side, and capture Jugurtha, leading to the end of the war. This action did garner him some attention — in fact, King Bocchus donated a statue of Sulla on horseback gilded in gold to be erected in the Roman Forum — but Gaius Marius took eventual total credit for it since Sulla was serving under him at the time of this action.

In 104 B.C.E., a group of migratory Germanic-Celts, made up of the Cimbri and Teutones, were heading towards Italy. Marius was appointed to lead the campaign against them, being seen as the best general in Rome after his victory over the Numidians. Sulla worked alongside him once again as a *tribunus militum*. However, about halfway through the campaign he was transferred to service under Catullus as his legate, a higher position. This was partially done because Catullus was known as an incredibly incompetent general who was terrible at working together with Marius. With Sulla's intervention, the two armies were able to work together, and the worst of Catullus' impulses were curbed. At the Battle of Vercellae in 101 B.C.E., the roving Germanic-Celtic army was destroyed and both Gaius and Catullus received triumphs and honors as the victorious co-commanding generals.

2 THE ROMAN REPUBLIC

"For although the Romans of that time no longer retained their ancient purity and uprightness of life, but had degenerated, and yielded to the appetite for luxury and extravagance, they nevertheless held in equal opprobrium those who lost an inherited wealth and those who forsook an ancestral poverty." -Plutarch, Life of Sylla

It is important to understand the context of any major historical figure's life, particularly if one hopes any insight into their world and motivations. The Roman Republic followed the Roman Kingdom and ended with the Roman Empire. The Roman Kingdom, the early, monarchical structure which founded Rome as a city and claimed many territories, ended in 509 B.C.E. when its leaders were overthrown by democratic revolutionaries. The Republic would end in 27 B.C.E. with the ascension of Augustus from consul to emperor. Society during this period was seen as a mix of Latin, Greek, and Etruscan elements, and its political organizations were largely influenced by Greek city-state examples. Society was led by two consuls, who were essentially the leaders of the state who were elected each year. In reality, their democracy worked out to more of an oligarchy, as only certain individuals could vote and only certain individuals (often from the aristocratic class) actually met the requirements to participate in an office.

The Roman Republic was in "a state of quasi-perpetual war throughout its existence." First, it had to battle the Latin and

Etruscan peoples who surrounded the area, slowly conquering them, and the Gauls even managed to sack Rome in 387 B.C.E before they were driven back. After the sack of Gaul, Rome conquered the entire Italian peninsula within one hundred years, which made the Republic a huge powerhouse within the Mediterranean. The absolute greatest enemy of the Republic was Carthage, with whom it fought three major wars. Once Carthage was finally defeated, Rome was unquestionably the power center of the region. The Republic was also marked by a series of violent civil wars and many political crises. Many of these related to the vast difference in population and rights between the patrician and the plebian classes and the impact that large numbers of slaves in the later empire had on the peasantry, middle class and urban workers. Oftentimes, particularly in the later republic, murder was used by people on every side to remove individuals who tried to push forward initiatives that were not to their liking. One of the major uprisings was of the slaves and led by Spartacus who managed to hold back and repeatedly defeat the Roman army for several years. The final years of the Republic — the years in which Sulla and his contemporaries lived and worked — were an absolute mess of murder, infighting, civil war, and grabs for power by various parties.

This text, of course, already covers many of those crises, or the ones that they would eventually lead to. So what was everyday life like for a Roman citizen? Families were headed by the oldest male member who was called the *paterfamilias* and had completely authority over property and family members. Citizenship gave an individual various rights, but one could be made "infamous" by which one would lose legal and social opportunities and privileges. Citizenship also came with taxation responsibilities and if you could not pay, there was a chance you could be executed, though if you could not pay in cash you might enter into a temporary debt bondage to pay off the debts. This sometimes happened with men giving their sons in service to someone whom they owed money to for a certain period of time. Slaves were both seen as members of the family and as property, but could buy their freedom after which point their sons would be eligible for citizenship. Slaves often earned money by doing odd jobs or trades for individuals outside of the family, or sometimes rendering skilled services for the family itself.

Both men and women could be citizens, and were supposed to marry and have as many children as they humanly could to improve their family's "wealth, fortune, and public profile." Patrician status was only inherited by birth; some attempts at various points were made to stop patrician-plebian marriages, but they tended to happen anyway. Oftentimes plebian women enjoyed more freedom than their patrician counterparts, though once widowed, women were no longer subjected to the will of their husband (instead, they remained subjected to the will of their father until his death) they all enjoyed a greater degree of day-to-day freedom. Under that system, when the father died, they were fully independent individuals. During this period — or the end of the republic — the birth rate among the elite began to fall rapidly. Many wealthy citizens turned to adoption to make sure they had heirs as well as to create further political alliances. Adoption could happen at any age in Rome, so oftentimes there were old men adopting fully adult males in order to make sure they inherited the property and position.

The Republic was largely agrarian focused around cereal crops and vegetables. Oftentimes, especially as time went on, the nobility turned more and more to using slaves to farm their land instead of hiring workers from the city or surrounding region. This caused a great loss of jobs for the more middle-class and lower-class Romans, forcing many to sell themselves into slavery simply to gain a place to live and jobs. Oftentimes the Republic had to turn to systems of subsidizing or providing free grain in order to keep the population fed until agricultural systems advanced enough that there was always a surplus. Eventually, Rome developed into a sort of "Bread Basket" for the area, supplying an abundance of crops to the Mediterranean area.

Much of Rome's mythology and religion was tied to its semi-mythic start, with Romulus and Remus founding Rome after a blessing from Jupiter. In reality, many of the gods were renamed and slightly altered versions of the Greek ones, as the Romans had no reservations about stealing ideas and ideology from the Greeks. Romans believed in a huge number of deities, and that the well-being of the state depended on the deities being kept happy and respected. As such, religious duty was seen as a very civic service, with less concern over individuals' actual beliefs in the practice. As long as a person showed respect to the gods in the prescribed ways and attended the festivals in their honor, it did not matter much what they did in their everyday lives. This allowed for the creation of many private, mystic, and secret cults, which tended to more spiritually and philosophically fulfill people's religious needs. The Roman state allowed the performance and existence of these cults as long as they did not interfere with one's ability to revere the state gods (Christianity would cause problems in the Empire, as reverence towards the state gods and the emperor was seen as heresy within that faith practice; the Roman leaders believed that by not revering the gods and emperor, the Christians were fundamentally putting the Roman Empire as a whole at risk).

For Sulla, once he gained riches, life would have been relatively easy. His family and his family slaves would have kept the house running while he spent his time at war or involved in the political goings-on in the Senate. In fact, slavery was considered crucial to the survival of democracy at the time, because it was believed that without slaves to carry out daily tasks no citizen man or patrician would have the free time necessary to participate in the many and constant political goings-on.

3 EARLY POLITICAL CAREER

"His personal appearance, in general, is given by his statues; a but the gleam of his gray eyes, which was terribly sharp and powerful, was rendered even more fearful by the complexion of his face. This was covered with coarse blotches of red, interspersed with white. For this reason, they say, his surname was given him because of his complexion, and it was in allusion to this that a scurrilous jester at Athens made the verse:—'Sulla is a mulberry sprinkled o'er with meal.'" - Plutarch, *Life of Sylla*

Sulla's appearance was recorded as "red-blond, blue-eyed, and...a dead-white face covered with red marks." Plutarch wrote that Sulla was quite proud of his blonde hair, believing that it gave him a "singular appearance". His personality was said to be two-sided; on one hand, he was known for being charming and having an easy sense of humor, seen as quite approachable by even the lowest of peons. However, when he was playing the role of general or dictator, he was known to be incredibly stern. This did not mean he was continuously harsh with his men - one of his army's favorite jokes to play was singing a song they composed about him having only one testicle. This was untrue, but Sulla allowed it, saying he was "fond of a jest". However, individuals never knew what to expect of him. Plutarch wrote that, "at the slightest pretext he might have a man crucified, but on another occasion would make light of the most appalling crimes; or he might happily forgive the most unpardonable offenses and then punish trivial, insignificant misdemeanors with death and confiscation of property." He was known throughout his life for engaging in "excesses" and "debauchery" which was explained by many historians as a result of losing his father at a young age and being in the hands of a doting step-mother who had no qualms about spoiling him. His poor upbringing made him able to interact with the plebeians in a way that many patricians were unable to, but it also led him to furiously pursue the rich life he had been denied as a child, at the expense of other poor people. Before his wars in his thirties, he had no real military knowledge, though some historians believe that along with significant intelligence it was likely his understanding of everyday psychology and poor soldier motivations that allowed him to be so successful. This would certainly explain his ability to convince enemy armies to join his own forces before a fight even took place.

After this military incursion, Sulla returned to Rome, where he was appointed *Praetor urbanus* in 97 B.C.E. A *praetor urbanus* was similar to a judge, and presided over civil cases between citizens. In the absence of consuls, who were in charge of the committee, the praeter would be in charge of the day-to-day operations and civic control of the Republic. Sulla was then the first Roman magistrate to meet with a Parthian ambassador, a man by the name of Orobazus. Later he took a seat between the Parthian ambassador and the Cappadocian ambassador. This slighted the Parthian ambassador because it seemed to portray the Parthians and Cappadocians as equals, which was not something the Parthians believed. Because of "allowing this humiliation," Orobazus was executed at his return to Parthia. Shortly thereafter, Sulla was told by a mystic seer from Chaldea that he "would die at the height of his fame and fortune". This fortune greatly impacted Sulla and he would carry it with him for the rest of his life, it influencing much of his actions and work. In 94 B.C.E., Sulla managed to successfully repel the forces of Tigranes the Great of Armenia from Cappadocia, keeping Rome safe as was his duty as *praetor urbanus*. Later that same year, Sulla aligned himself with the "optimates" political party in opposition to his old commander, Gaius Marius.

Optimates, a word which means "best ones", were the "traditionalist Senatorial majority of the late Roman Republic". They were the enemies of the Populares, or those "favoring the people," who took a more populist pro-plebeian stance. The Optimates wanted to limit the Tribune of the Plebes and extend the power of the Senate, which they believed would enhance the power of the patricians. They were also worried about individual generals rising up, backed by the people's tribune, taking control completely from the Senate and the aristocracy. Oftentimes, individuals who were a part of the optimates were not necessarily in it because they believed the aristocracy was inherently better than the plebian class, but because the advancement of the aristocracy advanced their own personal goals. Sulla was most certainly one of these individuals; his upbringing and continued consorting with the artistic classes belied that he held no personal hatred for plebians. However, his love of them was not strong enough for him to overlook personal gain in the face of their collective loss of power, class mobility, and general quality of life.

During the period of 91 B.C.E to 88 B.C.E., the Social War broke out. The Social War was a war between the Romans and the Socii, which were a collection of autonomous tribes and city-states within the Italian peninsula who had submitted to Roman law in exchange for certain amount of personal freedoms and rights, as well as the ability to rule their territories more or less as they saw fit. However, while similarly submitted groups like the Latins had long been allies of the Romans, the Socii had been Roman enemies until they were eventually conquered and absorbed into the empire. Because of this, they received considerably worse treatment than individuals like the Latins, who enjoyed higher respect from their Roman leaders.

Since the Socii were Roman subjects, they would often be called upon to act in arms and defend the Roman Republic from invaders (or serve in Roman military incursions against surrounding cultures). Additionally, they were forced to pay Roman taxes — usually much higher than what other subjected groups or Romans were forced to pay — but unlike Romans, they had no input on how these taxes were used or why and when armies and levies would be raised in their areas. Many individuals had tried on both sides for years to extend Roman citizenship to the Socii with no success. Some of the individuals who tried to extend rights from within the Republic were removed from power or, even more often, assassinated by optimates and other pro-Roman supporters; these individuals included people such as Marcus Livius Drusus the Younger who had tried to strengthen the Senate and make Roman citizenship universal. In response to this, and the continued felt injustices from the Republic, the Socii rebelled.

4 FIGHTING FOR POWER

> *"Sulla, on the other hand, did much that was memorable, and achieved the reputation of a great leader among his fellow-citizens, that of the greatest of leaders among his friends, and that of the most fortunate even among his enemies. But he did not feel about this as Timotheus the son of Conon did, who, when his adversaries ascribed his successes to Fortune, and had him represented in a painting as lying asleep, while Fortune cast her net about the cities, was rudely angry with those who had done this, because, as he thought, they were robbing him of the glory due to his exploits, and said to the people once, on returning from a campaign in which he was thought to have been successful: "In this campaign, at least, men of Athens, Fortune has no share.""* -Plutarch, Life of Sylla

At the start of the war the Roman aristocracy and Senate were becoming increasingly wary of Gaius Marius' ambition. He had proven again and again that he had no qualms about taking credit from others or removing his perceived opponents through any means necessary. He had already gained six consulships, five of which happened in a row from 104 B.C.E. to 100 B.C.E. and the Senate did not wish for him to have complete control of military forces throughout Italy. Sulla showed himself to be incredibly effective during this uprising, outshining Marius Gaius and Gnaeus Pompeius Strabo in 89 B.C.E. He managed to capture the chief town of the Hirpini, Aeclanum, by setting the outer regions of the city ablaze. This resulted in the surrender of the allied Socii and the conclusion of the Social War the following year. In reward, he was elected consul in 88 B.C.E., serving alongside Quintus Pompeius Rufus.

Besides the consulship, Sulla's service won him many more acclaims. One of these was the Corona Obsidionalis, also called the Corona Graminea or "Grass Crown". Received for his actions at the battle of Nola, it was the "highest Roman military honor, awarded for personal bravery to a commander who saves a Roman legion or army in the field." The actions needed for the award to be granted were different than for others; it required that the saved army forces nominate and acclaim the general for the award, so it was incredibly rare. The crown was woven from grasses or plants that were taken from the field of battle on which the heroic act took place.

As his first action of consul, Sulla was planning to head to the East of the republic to lead the fight in the first Mithridatic War against King Mithridates VI of Pontus. However, Marius Gaius was still scheming for power and wanted to lead the attack himself. So before his departure, Sulla and his co-consul Quintus Pompeius Rufus worked together to block legislation brought forward by tribune Publius Sulpicius Rufus which would have allowed for the rapid organization of all of the Italian Allies who had Roman citizenship. In response, Pompeius Rufus tried to have Sulla killed, forcing him into temporary hiding in a friend's house. Sulla's son-in-law was murdered in some of the riots this political maneuvering caused. As soon as Sulla left Rome to try and start the war, Sulpicius received news from Marius that if he acted more strongly against Sulla, his numerous debts would be forgiven. Sulpicius then called an assembly demanding that Sulla's consulship be revoked and given to Marius. Sulpicius used various assemblies to disqualify different Senators from the Senate until there were not enough Senators left to form a quorum, trying to force them to do as he said. A riot broke out in the Forum and noblemen attempted to lynch Sulpicius but were halted by his several gladiator bodyguards he had hired, out of fear it may come to this.

Sulla, at his war camp, received the news that Marius had been successful and the power of the consulship, as well as authority to administer the war, were going to be taken away from Sulla. Sulla's soldiers were as furious as he. The general then gathered six legions of his most loyal men and marched on Rome, something that had never happened before. No other leader had crossed the "*pomoerium*," or city limit, with his army before. All but one of his commanders, Lucullus, who was related to him through marriage, refused to cross the boundary with him. But Sulla argued that the Senate had been "neutered" and therefore *mos maiorum*, or "the way of the elders," (essentially the understood constitution, as Rome had no official one) was offended that the Senate had taken away the consul's right to fight the wars of the year of his leadership. The gladiators guarding Rome were no match for trained soldiers and Marius made a last-ditch effort offering freedom to any slave who would join him and fight against Sulla. Only three agreed to help him and he was soon forced to flee the city altogether with his few supporters.

Sulla went directly to the Senate and declared Marius and any of his supporters enemies of the state, or *hostes*. He then berated the Senate, justifying his own actions and playing the victim of civil leadership gone awry. Sulla knew that after the chaos the Senate would be feeling weakened, so before his return to the war camp he reorganized and bolstered the men serving therein so they would not only support him but be indebted to him. Then, before he was to return entirely to war, Sulla decided to attempt to hunt down the men who had tried to rob him of his power. Sulpicius, who had been so instrumental in moving the pawns for Marius, was betrayed and then murdered by one of his own slaves. Sulla freed the slave for performing this service for him, but then had him executed for the crime of betraying his master. Marius made it to Africa, where it was difficult for Sulla to follow. Sulla then moved to actually fight Mithridates at long last, and Marius began his plot to receive the consulship for a seventh time which the Sibyl had told him he would.

At the end of 87 B.C.E., Marius returned to Rome while Sulla was still at war with Lucius Cornelius Cinna by his side and took command of the city. He made all of Sulla's passed laws and reforms no longer valid and then officially exiled Sulla as an enemy of the state. Both Marius and Cinna were elected as the consuls for the years 86 B.C.E., but then Marius died two weeks later, leaving Cinna in charge of Rome.

In 87 B.C.E., Sulla landed at Dyrrachium in Illyria. Asia at this time was fully occupied by Mithridates' forces, being led by Archelaus. Sulla first set out towards Athens which was ruled at this time by Aristion, a tyrant puppet put in place by Mithridates. Lucullus, the general who had stayed by his side when he marched on Rome, was the chief of staff and negotiated with Bruttius Sura who was the Roman commander currently present in Greece. After their negotiations, Sura quickly supported Sulla's efforts, passing over his troops. At Chaeronea, Sulla met with ambassadors from all the major cities in Greece besides Athens and made it clear to them that he planned to drive Mithridates fully from Greece and all Asian provinces, and asking for their support. Leaving this meeting he headed for Athens. Upon arriving at the city, he constructed siege works surrounding both Athens and its port town Piraeus, cutting it off completely. He had Lucullus raise a fleet from any Roman allies in the eastern Mediterranean as an attack on Piraeus, as without access to it there would be no way for Athens to refresh their supplies. Sulla needed massive amounts of wood and earth. Huge earthworks were built and then Sulla razed all of the surrounding trees including the sacred groves of Greece which extended one hundred miles from Athens. Then, when he needed funds, he raided the sacred treasures of the temples and the Sibyls in the area, minting their money into coins. The quality of these coins was so fine, since they were made from the fanciest temple treasures and as such would be highly prized in circulation for years afterwards.

Despite these actions on his part, the siege seemed to have reached a stalemate and the men were getting anxious. Sulla simply bided his time. Meanwhile, in their mad grab for power Marius and Cinna had gone on a murderous rampage, and before long Sulla's war camp was full of Roman refugees, including his entire family. Athens began to starve and grain reached famine prices. The population in the city was surviving off of leather and grass. Athens attempted to impress Sulla with a delegation who went on about the glory of the city and why it should be preserved for cultural and artistic reasons, and Sulla dismissed them saying, "I was sent to Athens not to take lessons, but to reduce rebels to obedience." Shortly thereafter, his spies within the city keyed him into the fact that Ariston had been neglecting the Heptachalcum, which was part of the city's wall. Sulla immediately attacked it, bringing down nine hundred feet of wall between the Sacred Gates and the Gates of Piraeus. His warriors rushed the city, and at midnight a sack took place which was so violent that "blood was said to have literally flowed in the streets." Only at the point where two of his Greek friends and the Roman Senators arrived back at camp were they able to eventually calm him. He then attacked the port of Piraeus more intensely, during which time Archelaus escaped. In his pursuit, he burned Piraeus to the ground. He then headed towards the city-state of Boeotia to take down Archelaus' remaining armies.

Sulla quickly intercepted the Pontic Army and occupied a hill, Filoboletus, which was close to Mount Parnassus. It had plenty of wood and water (Sulla's razing forces had not yet reached these woods). Archaelaeus' army approached from the north towards Chaerona. It was gigantic, at one hundred and twenty thousand men, outnumbering Sulla's army's at least three to one. Archelaus wanted to wear the Roman army down, but Mithridates ordered him to attack at once. Sulla built an earthworks around the city of Parapotamii, with a deep ditch full of spikes, and occupied the city. He feinted a retreat to fool Archaelus and the enemy moved forward to try and attack by outflanking him. However, Sulla had artillery hidden behind the palisades and threw back Archeleaus' right wing. In the confusion, the enemy chariots charged Sulla's forces and were destroyed. The phalanxes could not pass the palisades and were destroyed by the Roman artillery. Archelarus' forces were continuously routed on each side, again and again, and some sources say that only ten thousand of the one hundred and twenty thousand survived. Sulla was not just victorious, he seemed like a god of war.

Cinna, still running Rome, then sent the commander Lucius Valerius Flaccus to relieve Sulla of his duty, still wanting to see him gone even after these victories. With Flaccus was a man named Gaius Flavius Fimbria who was known to be a layabout and general good-for-nothing. Eventually he would even try to mutiny and have Flaccus killed by his men, though that would fail. This new Roman force camped directly next to Sulla's bloodied and victorious one, and Sulla made short work of telling his troops to spread deceit and displeasure amongst the other troops. This tactic was so successful that many of Flaccus' men defected to Sulla's armies before Flaccus finally gave up trying to force Sulla off the path and headed north to attack Mithridates himself. Sulla made plans to intercept an incoming army.

He set up base in Orchomenus, a Boeotian town which had multiple defenses as the previous had. Sulla knew that once again he would be leading a smaller army facing down a significantly larger one and wanted to make sure things were in his favor as much as possible. This time, the attacking army would have over one hundred and fifty thousand men. The enemy army camped by a lake and slowly but surely Sulla had his men secretly build dikes, draining the lake out and around the enemy army and trapping them. Then, when they were fully surrounded by water, he attacked. Mithridates' forces had no way to get past the effective wall of Roman shields and swords and were slaughtered again. According to the ancient historian Plutarch, two hundred years later people were still finding armor and swords from the lake and surrounding area that had originated in this battle. This would end up being one of the most decisive battles; it would essentially solidify the idea of Rome's dominance in the mind of all of the surrounding peoples for the next thousand years.

5 ROAD TO ROME

"Then he set out from thence against Fimbria, who was encamped near Thyateira, and halting his army nearby, began to fortify his camp. But the soldiers of Fimbria came forth from their camp without any armour on, and welcomed Sulla's soldiers, and joined them eagerly in their labours, and when Fimbria saw this change in their allegiance, fearing that Sulla was irreconcilable, he laid violent hands on himself in the camp. Sulla now laid a public fine upon Asia of twenty thousand talents, and utterly ruined individual families by the insolent outrages of the soldiers quartered on them. For orders were given that the host should give his guest four tetradrachms a day, and furnish him, and as many friends as he might wish to invite, with a supper; and that a military tribune should receive fifty drachmas a day, and two suits of clothing, one to wear when he was at home, and another when he went abroad." -Plutarch, Life of Sylla

In 86 BC, after Sulla's victory in Orchomenos, he decided it would be best to head back to Rome, recapturing various Greek islands and city-states that had been claimed by Mithridates on his way. During this time, Flaccus would find troubles on his own end in regards to leadership and mutiny. At some point, as Flaccus' army crossed the Hellespont to pursue Mithridates' forces, Fimbria seems to have started a rebellion against Flaccus. While seemingly minor enough to not cause immediate repercussions in the field, Fimbria was relieved of his duty and ordered back to Rome. The return trip included a stop at the port city of Byzantium, however, and here Fimbria took command of the garrison, rather than continue home. Flaccus, hearing of this, marched his army to Byzantium to put a stop to the rebellion, but walked right into his own undoing. The army preferred Fimbria (not surprising considering his leniency in regard to plunder) and a general revolt ensued. Flaccus attempted to flee, but was captured shortly after and the consul was executed. With Flaccus out of the way, Fimbria took complete command.

In 85 B.C.E., the following year, Fimbria went to attack Mithridates directly while Sulla continued recapturing islands in the sea. Fimbria won a quick and decisive victory over Mithridatic forces: there were not many remaining after Sulla's continuous routs. However, he was unable to stop Mithridates' fleeing by sea. Fimbria then called on Lucullus', Sulla's right hand man, and asked him to use his fleet to create a blockade around Mithridates. However, Sulla had been scheming on his own behind everyone's back. In fact, he had been in negotiations with Mithridates to end the war without the rest of Rome knowing. He wanted it over with as quickly as possible so that he could finally return to Rome and reclaim power for himself. Lucullus thus refused to help Fimbria, and Mithridates appeared to "escape" to Lesbos, when in reality he was going to continue negotiations with Sulla.

Sulla, weirdly enough, offered relatively nice terms to Mithridates for the end of the war. There was no way — especially with Fimbria continuing to patrol and take back the islands — that Mithridates could ever claim any power. He was the absolute loser, and generally in these situations the victor would be harsh. But Sulla wanted to move things along. Mithridates had to officially give up his conquests which had already been taken from him, return any Roman prisoners he took, provide seventy ships to Sulla with supplies, and pay a tribute of three thousand gold talents. For this he would be able to keep his home kingdom and original territory that was not claimed through force and would regain his title as a friend of the Roman people. These terms were agreed to and the war seemed over.

Fimbria, however, was causing problems at sea. He was oppressing those both who had been fighting with Mithridates and those who were on the side of the Romans and Sulla. Sulla thus had to return to Asia and pursue Fimbria to his war camp, where Fimbria believed that he would be able to repel any attack from Sulla.

However, Fimbria's men did not want to face down the legendary general and the majority either refused to fight or defected to Sulla's side. Fimbria then took his own life, knowing there was no way he could win, and Sulla claimed the rest of the now dead man's army. He still had personnel issues; both his own forces and new ones were upset by how easily he had let Mithridates off, especially when he was known for taking harsh measures against all (as in the case of the slave who betrayed his enemy master). Sulla then started to penalize the Asian province, letting the veterans from his army extort wealth in the form of taxes and protection clauses. Fines were placed on almost every area for the cost of the war itself. This appeased many of the men who were then able to profit off of the conflict much more than their normal wages would have allowed.

Cinna was still in power at Rome and was facing issues with the Illyrian tribes under Roman control. Cinna raised his own army to try and fight this problem, and likely to prepare for what he knew would be issues arising when Sulla returned. The uprising was happening between Sulla's current location and the city, so Cinna was able to move his forces to Illyria in a defensive position that allowed him to guard against any attacks from Sulla while solving the insurgency issue. However, he had to force march his army through snowy mountains to reach the area, and they were incredibly unhappy with how he was running the entire operation. Not long into his new campaign, his men mutinied and stoned him to death. As soon as Sulla received word he knew he had to take advantage of the power vacuum Cinna's death had left behind and prepared five legions to march on Rome. He would leave two legions back in Asia Minor to keep the peace and protect against any peoples upset over the harsh levies and fines that had been placed on them.

In the spring of 84 B.C.E., Sulla set out and crossed the Adriatic with his fleet. No one met him as he landed which gave him plenty of time and room to establish camp and prepare for a new march on Rome. The city had already elected two new consuls - Cornelius Scipio Asiaticus and Norbanus. They raised their own armies to defend against Sulla and protect the Republican Senate against an individual who they felt would take over and declare himself the sole ruler of the city. Norbauns marched out first with the intent to block

Sulla from ever reaching Rome; however, Sulla easily routed him, and Norbauns was forced to retreat. Sulla followed him in his retreat and defeated him once again, completely exhausting the enemy army. During this time, Asiaticus marched south with his army. However, for some reason unknown from the sources, Asiaticus and/or his army did not seem to want to fight (which could have had entirely to do with Sulla's track record as a quick and vicious victor). Asiaticus set up a meeting with Sulla where they negotiated and he surrendered without fighting. His army then joined Sulla's, nearly doubling Sulla's forces. It also seems that Asiaticus was trying to set himself up as an ally to Sulla, or simply that he knew Sulla would win either way and wanted to do what he could politically and peacefully for the Republic. It is known that they had several long conversations about the state of the Republic and the importance of the democratic system, which may have been Asiaticus trying to influence him away from complete domination of the city.

Sulla also believed Asisaticus was fully on his side and did not keep him prisoner at the camp but let him free. He believed that Asiaticus would act as his messenger to the Senate. But for some reason the second Asiaticus was free he set about betraying Sulla and abandoned any idea of supporting him. While it was not surprising that Asiaticus did not actually have any loyalty to Sulla as a person, it seems smarter for one's survival to side with him at least temporarily. Sulla then declared that Asiaticus would suffer and die for betraying him, as would any man who tried to oppose him further. Many, hearing this and seeing his three victories that had just taken place, started to side with them. The first was the governor of Africa, Caecilius Metellus Pius. He led a revolt against any of Marius' remaining supporters in Africa. Picenum and Spain's leaders also turned to support him as did Marcus Licinius Crassus and Pompey who at this point had never held office and was only twenty three years old but managed to gather an army and appear, ready to take part in the new political happenings.

Asiaticus was suddenly ready to fight, in a strange turn of feeling. Perhaps what he and Sulla had discussed in terms of the future of the Republic had disturbed him so greatly he felt it necessary to make a stand. Asiaticus went after Pompey, but his army betrayed him and joined Pompey's forces. Asiaticus was stranded and abandoned. The Senate in Rome, desperate for a solution, re-elected Cinna's co-consul Papirius Carbo for his third term and Gaius Marius the Younger, the son of the disgraced dead consul who was twenty six years old. They started to recruit amongst the Italian tribes who had always been loyal to Marius and any others they believed would help, as well as setting on a campaign of murder against any of Sulla's supporters. Junius Brutus Damasippus, one of the praetors, personally led an attack on any senator who seemed in any way to favor the invading army, killing several.

At the start of the campaign year, at the beginning of spring 82 B.C.E., Carbo went with his forces to the north in order to fight Pompey while Marius the Younger moved to attack Sulla directly. Pompey could not be defeated and he and Metellus with African forces managed to take all of northern Italy for Sulla's cause. Marius the Younger recruited Samnites who feared that Sulla, with his aristocratic leanings, would take more power away from them if he reached the Senate. Marius and Sulla finally met at Sacriportus and it was a "long and desperate" battle. Eventually, Sulla again succeeded in one of his campaigns of persuasion and deceit, and over half of Marius' men defected to Sulla's army, forcing Marius to retreat. Sulla laid siege to the town he retreated to, Praeneste, and then left one of his generals in command of the attack while he moved north to attack Carbo who had retreated after his failed attacks on Pompey.

6 DICTATOR OF ROME

> *"Sulla now busied himself with slaughter, and murders without number or limit filled the city. Many, too, were killed to gratify private hatreds, although they had no relations with Sulla, but he gave his consent in order to gratify his adherents. At last one of the younger men, Caius Metellus, made bold to ask Sulla in the senate what end there was to be of these evils, and how far he would proceed before they might expect such doings to cease. "We do not ask thee,"* he said, *"to free from punishment those whom thou hast determined to slay, but to free from suspense those whom thou hast determined to save." And when Sulla answered that he did not yet know whom he would spare, "Well, then," said Metellus in reply, "let us know whom thou intends to punish." This Sulla said he would do."* -Plutarch, Life of Sylla

Neither Sulla nor Carbo managed to win a decisive victory, but Carbo knew that time was lost. Norbanus had defected to Sulla's side and Carbo found himself stuck between three enemy armies. He fled to Africa in defeat. There were some final Marian supporters; they gathered together and made multiple attempts to rescue Marius the Younger in Parneste, but Sulla's general stood firm. Pontius Telesinus was forced back from breaking the siege as well and finally moved north to attack Rome directly. In November of 82 B.C.E., Sulla's armies met Telenesius at the Battle of the Colline Gate outside of Rome. It was a huge battle with both sides believing that their victory would secure the proper future for Rome. Sulla's armies were forced back against the very walls of the city but Crassus, one of Sulla's generals, managed to turn against the opposition's flanks. The

Samnite and Marian forces broke and over fifty thousand men were killed between both sides. Sulla now had achieved his goal and defeated his enemies, gaining mastery of Rome.

Either immediately thereafter or within a few months the Senate made Sulla "dictator legibus faiendis et repibiclate constituendae causa" or the "dictator for the making of laws and for the settling of the constitution". The Assembly of the People, or Tribune Plebeian, approved the decision and did not place a term limit on his dictatorship. Dictatorships in the ancient world were often different than we think of them today, as it was usually an elected position (and was not always a position acquired through force as Sulla had done). Typically a dictator was elected for a short term of six months to a year during a time of political or military crisis. While this was a time of crisis, it was one that - in many ways - Sulla had orchestrated and caused. Sulla not had complete control of the republic of Rome and the city except for Hispania, which had been established under Marius' rule as an independent state. The circumstances of Sulla's appointment definitely made it an anomaly in previous versions of the dictatorship and many historians see Sulla as the precedent which Julius Caesar would follow, leading to the end of the Republic.

Sulla's first acts as dictator were a series of "proscriptions" which were programs executing any whom he believed to be an enemy of himself, and therefore the state, and then taking their property (which did not allow their heirs or remaining family to inherit it). According to Plutarch, "Sulla now began to make blood flow, and he filled the city with deaths without number of limit." Plutarch also claimed that many of the "enemies of the state" were not even enemies of Sulla or his administration, simply people that Sulla's supporters did not like, so he had them murdered to further curry the favor of his loyalists. Plutarch wrote, "Sulla immediately proscribed eighty persons without communicating with any magistrate. As this caused a general murmur, he let one day pass, and then proscribed two hundred and twenty more, and again on the third day as many. In an harangue to the people, he said, with reference to these measures, that he had proscribed all he could think of, and as to those who now escaped his memory, he would proscribe them at some future time."

Many historians see these killings as a direct response to the killings which Marius and Cinna had carried out while they ran the Republic during Sulla's absence fighting the war. Overall, Sulla carried out the death of at least one thousand five hundred nobles, and possibly a total of nine thousand people altogether, over the course of several months. If an individual murdered someone who had been "proscribed" they received two talents, which would be the equivalent to thousands of dollars today. However, if an individual tried to hide or shelter a proscribed person, they would also be executed. Because of this, "husbands were butchered in the arms of their wives, sons in the arms of their mothers." Even slaves could receive the rewards for murdering proscribed individuals, which would make it possible for them to buy their freedom, so in many ways the city went on the hunt. People knew who had been proscribed as public lists were posted in the Forum each day, updated with new names and with those who had been successfully killed removed after confirmation. Sulla could easily afford the large rewards given for murdering countrymen because the selling and auctioning of the dead's goods made him a profit, even after paying off murderers. In an attempt to protect himself in the future, Sulla also banned the sons and grandsons from running for political office. This rule would not be removed for over thirty years.

Gaius Julius Caesar, the famed Julius Caesar of history, was actually on Sulla's proscription list, as he was Cinna's son-in-law. He fled Rome and was rescued by relatives who hid him until finally Sulla spared him. However, Sulla wrote that he later regretted sparing the young, future dictator because he believed "he would become a danger to them in the future" and said, "In this Caesar there are many Mariuses."

Sulla, as mentioned previously, was an optimate on the side of strengthening the Senate. He instituted (or re-instituted) various reforms, including requiring Senatorial approval of any bill before it was submitted to the Plebeian council and restoring the "Servian" constitution of the Centuriate Assembly, or the Assembly of Soldiers. The Servian constitution introduced a census of all male citizens which established their wealth, military obligations, tax liabilities, and how significant his vote was in the process. It essentially made all citizens responsible for the military defense of the state and allied political and military life. He greatly hated the Plebeian Tribune position, or leader of the Plebeian Council - an important office, and only Senatorial office, that someone born to the plebian class could hold - because it was plebeian tribunes in the past who had robbed him of his power. He altered the duties of the position so that the Plebeian Tribune could no longer initiate legislation and banned individuals who had previously held the office to hold any others (after an individual held the title of Plebeian Tribune, occasionally it was possible for them to move up the ranks). Hey also made it impossible for the tribunes to veto Senatorial acts, up until this point one of their most important duties, though they were still allowed to act individually to protect specific Roman citizens.

Sulla increased the number of magistrates who would be elected each year and required any newly elected "quaestors", public officials who could hold a variety of roles, to be automatically admitted into the Senate. This allowed Sulla to change the size of the Senate from three hundred individuals to six hundred individuals. Sulla took the power and control of the courts from the equites, who had held it for hundreds of years, and transferred it to the Senators instead. Equites were a plebian class, technically, but acted more like a middle class in terms of wealth and prestige. Sulla established the law of *cursus honorum*, which codified the age and level of experience an individual needed to have before they were able to run for any certain office. He also wanted to make sure that no one tried to force him out of power in the same way he had gained it, so he put a ten year waiting period that an individual must respect before they were re-elected to office. He also changed the law so that consuls served in Rome during their year in office and then were given control of a provincial army and governorship for the year following it, placing him in charge of the military.

Then, in his boldest move as of yet, Sulla officially extended the "*Pomerium*", or "sacred boundary of Rome", a line which had not been altered since its establishment by Rome's early kings. And yet, Sulla was still strangely a traditionalist. Despite the fact that he had been elected to dictator with no term limit, at the end of 81 B.C.E. he resigned from office, disbanded his army, and enforced once again the consulship style of government. He then ran for office with Metellus Pius as co-consul and won for the year of 80 B.C.E. He dismissed all of his bodyguards and was known to walk freely around the city unguarded, offering to speak to any citizen who wished to explain his reforms and why he felt they were necessary for the betterment of Rome. Julius Caesar, later, would ridicule Sulla for resigning the dictatorship; he could not understand how a man would hand absolute power away.

7 LATER YEARS & LEGACY

"By this mode of life he aggravated a disease which was insignificant in its beginnings, and for a long time he knew not that his bowels were ulcerated. This disease corrupted his whole flesh also, and converted it into worms, so that although many were employed day and night in removing them, what they took away was as nothing compared with the increase upon him, but all his clothing, baths, hand-basins, and food, were infected with that flux of corruption, so violent was its discharge. Therefore he immersed himself many times a day in water to cleanse and scour his person. But it was of no use; for the change gained upon him rapidly, and the swarm of vermin defied all purification." -Plutarch, Life of Sylla

After the conclusion of his second year as consul, Sulla retired to his family's country villa in Puteoli with his wife and his long-time male lover, the actor Metrobius. Plutarch the historian is confused and dismissive of this relationship saying, "although Metrobius was past the age of youthful bloom, Sulla remained to the end of his life in love with him, and made no secret of the fact." Sulla, for the most part, stayed out of the political scene, only intervening when called up or he felt it absolutely necessary. Instead he focused on writing his autobiographical memoirs which he finished in 78 B.C.E., shortly before his own death. Tragically, they have been largely lost to us, with only a few fragments and references remaining in the writings of other authors. It would have been incredibly helpful to understand this interesting man's life and actions if we had the direct insight into his own mind. It is unclear exactly how Sulla died, though it seems to have either been from liver failure or a ruptured gastric ulcer, possibly due to "chronic alcohol abuse", though there is a chance that he died from a worm infestation also caused by the ulcers.

Sulla's funeral was a giant, public affair in the Roman Forum, and would not be matched in grandiosity until the death of the first Roman Emperor Augustus in 14 C.E. His body was carried into the city on a golden bier surrounded by the men who had served in his armies and eulogies were given by prominent Senators at the time, including Lucius Marcius Philippus, who gave the main funeral oration. His body was then cremated and placed in a tomb in the Campus Martius. Sulla had written his own inscription before his death which read, "No friend ever served me, and no enemy ever wronged me, whom I have not repaid in full."

Sulla had a radical and lasting impact on Roman history. Many historians see him as the true beginning of the fall of the Republic; while the Republic had been struggling for many years with internal fighting, murderous plots, and dissolution of powers in different areas, it still seemed possible to many that it could be re-centered on the right track. However, Sulla set the example that an individual could successfully seize total power - and even be rewarded for it afterwards with another elected position. Pompey is quoted saying, "If Sulla could, why can't I?" And this idea certainly carried out for aspiring Senators in the following years. Sulla had also not established a method by which the army would be more loyal to the Senate and the state instead of individual generals, essentially giving any powerful consul or leader his own personal army. He did try to pass laws that limited the actions of generals, but when a man has an army at his back he is less likely to follow his own boundaries of power. While some of his laws, like those concerning generals' actions and the regulations on governorships would endure for a significant period of time into the Roman Principate, the majority of his reforms were repealed within ten years after his death. Understandably, the veto ability of the Plebian tribunes and their ability to bring forward legislation was rapidly reinstated. Sulla's family would remain very powerful moving forward, even into the Empire. His son Faustus Cornelius Sulla would issue money bearing Sulla's name, a definite power move during the time, as would his grandson Quintus

Pompeius Rufus. Various descendants, including Lucius Cornelius Sulla in 5 B.C.E, Faustus Cornelius Sulla in 31 C.E., Lucius Cornelius Sulla Felix in 33 C.E., and Faustus Cornelius Sulla Felix in 52 C.E. would hold consulships in the empire. The final, Faustus Felix, would end up marrying the daughter of emperor Claudius, Claudia Antonia. However, he would be executed in 62 C.E. by Emperor Nero, which would end the Sulla line.

Sulla, like many prominent Romans during the Republic, would have several wives (divorce was not viewed as a negative or scandalous thing during this time). His first wife was either named Ilia or Julia, and may have been related to Julius Caesar, quite possibly being Julia Caesaris, Caesar's first cousin once removed. Together they would have two children,. Cornelia and Lucius Cornelius Sulla. Cornelia would first marry Quintus Pompeius Rufus the Younger and later Mamercus Aemilius Lepidus Livianus, the mother of Pompeia, who would become the second wife to Julius Caesar. Lucius Cornelius Sulla, sadly, would die young. His second wife was Aelia and they seem to not have had children. His third wife was Cleolia, and Sulla would divorce her for her inability to have children. HIs fourth wife was Caecilia Metella who would give birth to Faustus Cornelius Sulla and Cornelaia Faustua, who would marry Gaius Memmius and then Titus Annius Maelo. She would give birth to Gaius Memmius, who was a consul in 35 B.C.E. His fifth and final wife was Valeria, who would give birth to Cornelia Postuma after Sulla's death.

Sulla has been referenced often in literature and cultural media due to his huge impact on the Roman Republic. He is the main character of four different Italian operas, two of which - it should be noted- take considerable creative liberty with his actual life and history. In both Lucius Sill by Mozart and Silla by George Frideric Handel he is shown to be a ruthless, blood-obsessed womanizer and tyrant who eventually has a great moment of repentance, explaining his abdication of the dictatorship. Pasquale Anfossi and Johan Christian Bach wrote slightly less exaggerated operas on his life. He is also a main character in the first three of Colleen McCullough';s Masters of Rome novels, a series of historical fictions.

Sulla

Printed in Great Britain
by Amazon